MARTY FIELDS

SHORT JOKES FOR TALL PEOPLE

WP

Published by:
Wilkinson Publishing Pty Ltd
ACN 006 042 173
Level 4, 2 Collins Street
Melbourne, Vic 3000
Ph: 03 9654 5446
www.wilkinsonpublishing.com.au

National Library of Australia Cataloguing-in-Publication entry

Creator: Fields, Marty, author.

Title: Short jokes for tall people / Marty Fields.

ISBN: 9781925642018 (paperback)

Subjects: Fields, Marty–Humor.
         Australian wit and humor.

Cover design by Matt Irwin
Internal design by Spike Creative Pty Ltd
Richmond, Victoria. Ph: (03) 9427 9500
spikecreative.com.au

CONTENTS

DEDICATION

My thanks firstly go to my family, Jenny and Hayley, for making me feel valued and special and loved. And to my mum, who I just lost, who was an absolute cornucopia of knowledge about comedy and brought me up beautifully despite never having had a lesson. For my late father who showed me how to treat people and also for his love. For Stella and Rose, our family pets who make me smile. For all my mates in the industry, Ken Murdoch, Grantlee O'Sullivan, Dan and Tony at the Comics Lounge and all the comics I've laughed with over the years, especially the late Haskel Daniel.

This book is also for anyone not in the business who has decided it's a good thing to try and make someone else laugh.

MY HERITAGE

I was born into a comedy family. My father, Maurie Fields, and my mother, Val Jellay, were working on a weekly television variety show when I came into the world. Mum worked in very physical comedy sketches while pregnant with me, which may explain my appearance.

They had both come from long careers in the industry.

After playing in his mum's jazz band, Dad joined a comedy and musical duo called Skit and Skat, playing the Sydney clubs. Mum had starred in the Tivoli theatre circuit as a "straight woman", or foil, working with all the comedy greats of the time. She then went to England and Europe, playing in shows right across the continent. When she came back to Australia, she was asked to direct a huge touring vaudeville and variety show called Sorlies Revue Company. It was like The Great Moscow Circus, in a tent but huge.

Dad and his partner auditioned for her and she hired them, eventually teaching him how to be funny. After seven years of travelling Australia with Sorlies, they came to Melbourne to do *Sunnyside Up*, and settled down to raise a family, which was me.

Mum retired from the industry to raise me, but dad just got bigger and bigger, both as an actor and a comedian.

Eventually Mum and Dad reunited on camera to play the owners of the pub in the long running drama, *The Flying Doctors*. All the while, dad was working the comedy circuit and eventually found a home on the popular TV show, *Hey Hey it's Saturday*. I joined him on the show on 1992 until his death in 1995. After his death, I continued on the show.

Mum went on to write four fantastic books on show business and comedy in general. She continued to do guest speaking roles until her death in 2017.

They were both giants of the industry and are sorely missed.

So here I am, carrying on that legacy.

It's not a heavy burden as they taught me well. I hope you agree.

FOREWORD

Thanks for buying the book. And if you're just reading this without having bought the book yet, this is not the best part. The best part is actually buying the book. So go on.

This is my fourth comedy book. My last one, *Funny Things*, was a cracker. If you didn't read it, try and find it. I'll wait.

In the meantime, here's a little about this book, me and comedy in general.

I was born into show business and comedy. My mum was pregnant with me while doing a weekly live comedy/variety TV show. I grew up around funny people. People who knew just what to say and how to say it to make it funny.

These days folks often say to me, "How come when I say something, it's not funny but when you say the same thing, it is?" The purists would tell you it's about timing, word emphasis and that stuff. But the parallel I draw is this: If you're an Australian but have Greek parents and you grow up around a Greek accent, you're going to have a Greek accent, despite never having been to Greece. Well I grew up around comedians. My mum and dad were both very funny so I developed a comedy accent. Just knowing instinctively how to say something to make it funny.

I'd like to say my humour got me out of a lot of tight situations but it was usually the reason I was in those situations in the first place. Always knowing just what not to say at the perfect time was a bad habit of mine. My wife says I'm "ready, fire, aim" when talking to people. She's right although I'd like to think I'm getting better.

I've been in the entertainment industry full time my whole life. Everything I have is the product of performing in one medium or another. I hear that's unusual. I've actually only had one job outside the business, and that was a two week stint as a storeman and packer which went, um, poorly. I was around people there who had no interest in laughing and having a good time which was completely foreign to me. They didn't like me either because I wasn't like them. But I was used to that. My entire childhood I'd been the odd one out.

I grew up in a poor area of Melbourne, went to a tough school for my first thirteen years before eventually finding my way to a private school where I actually learnt how to conduct myself. I was finally around people who appreciated humour and I blossomed, if a straight boy can "blossom".

I was a classically trained pianist, doing 15 years of practical and music theory at the Melba Conservatorium. By age 14, I was working at pubs playing piano, singing and telling old jokes from behind the piano. I toured as Musical Director for *Snow White and the Seven Dwarves* around Australia for ten years, I acted in heaps of TV dramas from a very early age, I've done twelve professional musicals, winning best acting awards, I've done five years of talkback radio in Melbourne and blah blah blah, I'd like to thank the Academy. I've done lots of stuff and by my age you'd expect that. I'm not going to drag you through my CV. The point is that all of that eventually led to me standing alone at a mic telling gags. Looking back it seemed to make sense I'd finish up there, which is where I feel I belong. It's a great job. But looking forward, back then, I had no idea where my future lay.

I've made some great friends over the years. My best friend, Ken, is a guitarist. My other best mate runs a comedy club,

The Comics Lounge. I have a lot of mates at the Comics Lounge in Melbourne. It's a great hub for standup in Australia and was recently voted the 7th best comedy club in the world, which is kind of cool. I have a beautiful wife who keeps finding new ways to tolerate me, an amazing daughter who keeps me on my toes and never lets me think I'm remotely cool, a dog, a cat and a lot of inflatable fruit.

The book you're holding is a collection of lots of things. Jokes I've used on stage and jokes I've heard that I liked but aren't being used by anyone I'm aware of. Most jokes are new, some are old, and that's ok because there's no such thing as an old joke if you haven't heard it. And jokes only hang around and get old if they're funny. These gags are definitely edgier than I've given you in the past. But I think they're funny. If you're offended by one, that wasn't my intention. Just move on. You'll be ok.

So where am I now? It's been 50 years since I did my first gig on the ABC at age 6. That's a long time to exist in the bizarre world of show business. Am I happy? I suppose if a performer can ever be truly happy, I guess they need to be comfortable with where they've gotten to in the business and despite a lifetime of trying, I'm still not quite there. I don't know what "there" is but that's the great thing about this industry. You never know what's around the corner. And despite that being absolutely terrifying, I kind of like it.

I hope you enjoy the book.

Cheers, Marty.

HOW TO WRITE OR TELL A JOKE

It's reasonably easy to write your own jokes or tell gags you've heard, as long as you follow a few basic guidelines.

1. First of all, don't add unnecessary details. Unless it's pivotal to the tag. (The tag is the funny part at the end. "Punchline" is sometimes used but it's an American term for tag.) It doesn't matter what the weather was like, or how she looked or what time it was. Longer is not usually funnier. Get on with it.

2. Don't add swear words if you don't need them. They're distracting.

3. Choose your audience. Don't try to offend people who don't want to be offended.

4. Talk about things your audience already know about. It's no use telling someone about the food in Belgium if they've never been to Belgium. It's no use telling a farmer an airline joke. They don't fly much. You get the idea.

5. Make the first sentence funny or weird enough to capture their attention.

6. And finally, don't laugh at your own joke. Laugh at the audience if they don't get it.

HOW TO PUT TOGETHER A SPOT OR GAG ROUTINE

1. Start the set off with your funniest short joke.

2. Finish the set off with your funniest long joke.

3. Make everything in the middle hilarious. What I mean by that is, if a joke is not great, don't use it just to fill your time. You're better finishing early than losing the crowd with a lame gag.

4. Go to the crowd with your content. Don't try and drag them to you or you'll spend half your set explaining what you're talking about. Don't talk to old people about drugs or the internet. Don't talk to young people about doctors, having kids etc. It's so much easier to get a laugh if the audience is with you on the topic.

5. Don't lash out with your jokes. People these days are desperate to be offended. Make your material primarily self-debasing. It's hard to get pissed off at a comedian who is bagging themselves.

6. And finally, be likeable on stage. This is so important. An audience will laugh at you if they like you.

SHORT JOKES FOR TALL PEOPLE

Welcome to Autopsy Club. As you know, it's Wednesday, which is open Mike night.

I wonder if sausage dogs are made from all the leftover bits of other dogs.

Probably my earliest memory is being 28 and surviving that head injury.

I bought a book on eBay called 'How to scam idiots on eBay'.

That was three months ago, and it still hasn't arrived.

My wife told me "Sex is better on holiday". Worst postcard ever.

For sale:
Pack of tic tacs.
Unopened.
Mint condition.

The guy who stole my diary has died.
My thoughts are with his family.

I married my wife for her looks. But not the ones she's been giving me today.

I just got asked the time by a Telstra serviceman. I told him it was between 8am and 1pm.

If at first you don't sucseed, succeedd, suxeedd ... oh, screw it.

Me: Waiter, my wife knocked her drink over.

Waiter: No problem, I'll get you another one.

Me: Thanks. Make sure the next one likes footy.

I've applied for a job as an Echo. I'm just waiting to hear back from them.

A woman weightlifter goes to the doctor. "I've been taking so many steroids I've grown a dick."

The doctor said, "Anabolic?"

She said, "No, just a dick".

Kim Kardashian was robbed of $14m in jewellery. The thieves eventually took the jewels after unsuccessfully searching her for any talent.

Mama Mia: a classic Abba song about an Aussie boy telling his mother he's arrived.

My wife said she's sick of the way I always get my directions mixed up.

So I packed my bags and right.

If you rearrange the letters of "Postmen", they get very annoyed.

The TV show *Casualty* is up to season 32! And to keep it true to life some of the patients from season one are just being seen.

Shania Twain has announced the birth of her son, 'Choo Choo'.

Beethoven was so deaf he thought he was a painter.

Parliamentarians would probably get along a lot better if they agreed never to bring up politics.

It's always difficult when someone close to you passes away.

The best strategy is to just ask the flight attendant if you can move seats.

I bet centaurs never know who to barrack for at rodeos.

I want to get another parrot but I can't because I don't have a parrot.

I've been cycling to get fit but people say it makes me look ridiculous.

So to macho up my image I've drawn some racing stripes on my basket.

I just had forty winks on the train. I knew I shouldn't have worn this pink floral shirt.

I've been taking Viagra for my sunburn.

It doesn't cure it, but it keeps the sheets off my legs at night.

My wife has just left me because of my obsession with horse racing.

She's in the yard, she's at the gate ... and she's off!

Two cops just knocked on my door during my party. They said, "We've been getting complaints."

I said, "Then start doing a better job."

At an interview:

First question: "Describe yourself
in three words."

Me: "Not good with numbers."

———————————

I think the guy that started IKEA's favourite
part of his school day was assembly.

———————————

I suppose I better get up and hit the gym.

Stupid autocorrect, I meant gin.

———————————

I can count the number of times I've been
to Chernobyl on one hand.

It's seven.

———————————

My mate just rang me and said,
"What are you doing at the moment?"

I said, "Probably failing my driving test."

———————————

Seen the new $5 note? The government
says they'll last longer, but I bought a
coffee at the airport and it was gone.

———————————

I joined a club for people with Tourette's Syndrome. It took 4 hours to get sworn in.

James Bond would be a much better spy if he didn't keep telling everyone who he was.

One of the worst jobs around the house my wife gets me to do is clean the poo out of the kitty litter tray. It's bad 'cause we don't own a cat.

At the Fashion awards:

"And the prize for best neck wear goes to ... well would you look at that, it's a tie!"

I went to our local Chinese restaurant and got a free meal.

They do it for everyone who jumps out of the toilet window and runs off.

I rang the Paranoia Society. They said, "How the hell did you get this number?"

It was bad enough that Lance Armstrong was taking drugs. But he was also pedalling.

I never finish biographies. I can basically tell you where most famous people lived until they were six.

"You haven't listened to a word I've said, have you?" always seems like a strange way for my wife to start a conversation.

My mate bought a jigsaw puzzle at IKEA. Good luck putting that together.

I'm doing shift work at a factory making chess sets. I'm on Knights next week.

Welcome to Cosmetic Surgery Club. I see a lot of new faces here tonight.

According to NASA, you will be able
to see Jupiter and Saturn until April.

They also said that with a mirror,
you can see Uranus any time.

———————————————

I just bought 'Ventriloquism For Dummies'.

———————————————

The trickiest thing about trying to
name a baby is realising how many
people you hate.

———————————————

I was at Chemist Warehouse and a big box
of Omega 3 capsules fell on my head.

Luckily my injuries are superfishoil.

———————————————

I had an uncle with one leg who used to
work in a brewery. He was in charge of
the hops.

———————————————

I think tropical fish are a great pet if your
goal is to teach children about death.

———————————————

I'm making a fruit salad and the recipe
says "Pineapples — 5 cubed".

Where am I going to get 125 pineapples?

So many pigs seem to die while
eating an apple.

My wife asked me to bring home stuff
for the pancakes.

She wasn't happy when I arrived with
a push-up bra.

Google is 18 years old. Typical teenager.
Got an answer for everything.

My wife and I are having a competition
to see who can steal the most stuff from
the pet shop.

I've just taken the lead.

Keith Richards is what happens if Johnny
Depp rolls under your stove and you don't find
him until you pull the stove out months later.

Bi-Lo frozen lasagne is so horrible, the serving suggestion on the box is just a picture of it in a bin.

My wife is complaining that I never buy her jewellery.

To be fair, I didn't even know she sold jewellery.

I went to a swingers party where everyone dressed in army uniforms.

We had to leave our khakis in a bowl.

My wife said I'm trying to be someone I'm not.

I'm still confused how she got into the Batcave.

Interesting animal fact: If a dog is a police dog he has to tell you or it's entrapment.

I gave blood in February. I know it's not the usual Valentine's Day gift for your wife but it came from the heart.

I spent some time at my Auntie's grave today. Bless her. She thinks I'm digging a pond.

They say makeup sex is the best but I must be doing it wrong. I've got a lipstick stuck up my arse.

I'm waiting at the vet with my dog. A guy opposite me is weeping with an empty cage in his arms.

I'd be crying too if I were that forgetful.

Dentist: I'm sorry but this will hurt.

Patient: OK. Go for it.

Dentist: I used to bang your mum.

I'm sitting here wondering why the book I ordered, 101 ways to kill a postman, still hasn't arrived.

President Trump will meet with China's leader this week.

Topic of discussion: Walls and how to make them great.

———————

I'm reading the uncensored writings of Sir Arthur Conan Doyle, and it actually says, "No shit Sherlock!"

———————

Does technology make us happier?
I say no, but Siri tells me I'm mistaken.

———————

They say walking is the best exercise according to the guys who repossessed my car.

———————

I had a teacher who used to tell us to "Question authority".

I remember thinking, "Who the hell is he to tell me to question authority?"

———————

David Blain isn't a magician. What tricks does he do? "Ooh, I'm in a box and I'm not gonna eat!" That's no trick! That's housing commission.

———————

Job interviewer: "What are your strengths?"

Me: "I fall in love easily."

Job interviewer: "Okay ... what are your weaknesses?"

Me: "Those blue eyes of yours."

I took my wife to meet my parents.

"Son, I think this one's a keeper."

"Awww dad, what makes you say that?"

"She smells of monkey shit."

One of life's scariest creatures is a woman who calmly says "wow" during an argument.

A 7-Eleven was robbed by a man dressed as a mummy. Police described the suspect as 170cm, medium build and between 25 and 8,000 years old.

A kid was staring at me and his mum said, "That's what you'll look like if you only eat coco pops" and the kid started crying.

My grandpa fought in the war and survived mustard gas and pepper spray.

He was a seasoned veteran.

There's a miniature village in Melbourne's Fitzroy gardens.

One of the tiny houses caught fire and the flames could be seen up to a metre away

---

Today I met a girl with 12 nipples.
Sounds weird, dozen tit.

I've been charged with killing a man with sandpaper. It was an accident.

I was only going to rough him up a bit.

Girls mature faster than guys.
Men don't usually develop breasts
until their mid forties.

God: How many animals do I have
left to make?

Angel: Two.

God: How many legs do I have left?

Angel: One hundred.

Centipede: I call dibs!

Snake: Damn.

I just invented a new drink. It's 4 ounces
of stale black coffee served in a filthy
ashtray.

I call it "Breath of a Salesman".

Spiderman is a superhero because no one
else can shoot a sticky white substance
out of their body in public without everyone
freaking out.

My wife said she's leaving me because
I'm over-competitive.

I raced to the front door and yelled
"Not if I leave you first!"

My Old English Sheepdog's fur
is so matted he doesn't have fleas,
he has moths.

Beards are back in fashion. I have a beard.
Just not on my face.

I'm so broke if somebody robbed me they'd
just be doing it for the practice.

I bet Noah's wife said to Noah:
"Don't let the elephants watch what
the rabbits are doing".

My wife never lies about her age. She tells
everyone she's the same age as me.

Then she lies about my age.

I haven't seen my mate since he created
his own clone a year ago.

I wonder what he's been doing with himself.

Kettle's Salt & Vinegar Chips suggested serving size: Eat until your mouth starts to bleed.

I'm not happy with this new cooking spray.

I've used almost a whole can and my food is nowhere near done.

I got a rescue dog from the lost dogs home. I named it Karma. And by the name you'd think Karma was a male but no, Karma's a bitch.

I just bought a new garden trimmer.
It's cutting hedge technology.

I had insomnia so bad, the sheep fell asleep.

Just because nobody complains doesn't mean all parachutes are perfect.

I play online scrabble when I'm sitting on the toilet. Or as I call it, Turds with Friends.

If life is getting you down try drinking 2 litres of water before going to bed.

It'll give you a reason to get up in the morning.

There's a new record holder for the world's biggest egg, 7.4 kilos! That'll take some beating.

I wish I could be ugly for one day. Because being ugly every day sucks.

What do prison and the shift key have in common? They both turn your "o" into an "O".

Movies that stink:

Die Hard Boiled Eggs.

The Last Air Freshener.

There's Something About Mary's Arse.

No Showers For Old Men.

I just saw a sign that made me piss myself.
It said "Bathroom Closed".

A tuna fisherman was killed after
1200 kilos of fish fell on him.

Ironically he'd just won an argument about
fish being good for you.

My first car wasn't great. It was a Golf.
But I called it a Golf Ball because I couldn't
drive it more than 200 metres.

The doctor told my wife she was feeling
light-headed from a low iron level.

So to help her, I've raised the ironing board
up a bit.

I bumped into one of my old classmates
today. Thinning hair, beer belly, grey
moustache.

She's really let herself go.

The worst words you can hear at a concert are, "Ok, this is from our new album".

_____

I have two tickets for the A-League soccer if anyone wants to see me rip up two tickets to the A-League soccer.

_____

Unimaginative children play remake believe.

_____

Ever had a car splash water on you and you can't decide whether or not to go home for dry clothes?

So while you decide I'm gonna drive by you again.

_____

What separates us from the animals is that my litter box is the blue one.

_____

We've got a mouse problem despite having a cat. So I had to fire the cat.

He was sad but I told him, "Don't worry. You'll land on your feet".

_____

Is China really the most populated country in the world or did the same people get counted a few times?

In the army, I wonder why commandos aren't allowed to wear underwear.

Oh hi Lisa who wouldn't kiss me in spin the bottle in 6th grade and now wants to play Words with Friends. Seems the tables have turned, huh?

Guards at Barwon prison won't let inmates read the prison newspaper.

Ninety per cent of the paper is personal ads titled "Man Seeking Bitch".

A focus group have said they think Victorian Premier, Daniel Andrews, is distant and aloof.

Mr. Andrews could not be reached for comment.

I learned to fight from my dog. If I get attacked I throw myself on my back, put my legs in the air and encourage them to sniff my crotch.

I saw *Crouching Tiger, Hidden Dragon*. Disappointing. I didn't see one tiger or dragon.

Then I realised they were all crouching and hiding.

A chef in Belgium has killed his best friend and cooked his body parts.

This low-carb craze is really getting out of hand.

Anyone want to swap some arse jokes? I've got piles.

Saw Vincent van Gogh in a pub and asked if he wanted a drink.

He said, "No thanks, I've got one 'ere".

Two illegal employees at a Footscray Chinese Restaurant were caught bathing in the kitchen sink. And they still didn't wash their hands.

If my dog, Spot, is diagnosed with cataracts, I'm going to call him Blind-Spot.

Fun Fact: a good way to clean a toilet bowl is with Tang, the powdered space drink.

And as a bonus, your dog will feel like an astronaut.

I just tried to make a reservation at that cafe at the library but they were fully booked.

Wait, unicorns aren't real?
Are you saying I just blew a regular horse?

My father only hit me once.
But he used a Toyota.

Why are old maps always burnt around the edges?

"Shit. Larry's on fire! Put him out with that map!"

———————————

My wife said if I didn't do page 7 of the Kama Sutra she'd leave me.

It put me in a very difficult position.

———————————

I just bought the DeLorean from *Back to the Future* at an auction.

It was pretty expensive so I'll probably only drive it from time to time.

———————————

A piece of sandpaper walks into a bar. The bartender says, "What'll it be?" The sandpaper says, "Just something to take the edge off".

———————————

Can somebody come over here and hold my tits while I shake up this paint can?

———————————

According to my therapist, I have trouble focusing on blah blah blah ...

———————————

I got invited to speak at my old school. I can't believe Brighton Grammar took me back after 40 years. My mum must have written one hell of a sick note.

My wife said that she wants a divorce because of my obsession with cats.

I said, "I can't believe you're kicking meeeoowt".

"It's a boy!" I shouted, tears rolling down my face. "I don't believe it. A boy!"

And right then I decided I'd never visit Thailand again.

For the past 20 years, I've had a Valentine's card from a secret admirer but sadly I didn't get one this year. First my Nanna dies, now this!

It's International Women's Day tomorrow so to celebrate I got my wife a new bag and a new belt. The Hoover's as good as new now.

I've got a sister who works for the water board if you wanna meter.

Candle flames smell of burnt nose hair.

My life changed after I learnt Morse Code. Last night I couldn't fall asleep because the rain on the roof kept telling me it was going to kill me.

I took my daughter to KFC for the first time. I asked her what she wanted.

She asked, "What do you normally get when you come here?" I said, "Diarrhoea".

If a petrol station is on the right side of the road it might as well be on the moon.

Money's so tight at the moment that my wife is having sex with me because she can't afford batteries.

I thought I'd caught my neighbour spying on me with her binoculars tonight.

But it was just my reflection in her bedroom window.

"Our first categories tonight are supporting actors, which is what most actor's parents are still doing, supporting actors."

I've learnt the Mario Brother's strategy with anything.

"You try till you get killed then I'll have a go."

I'm not sure about our youth detention system. Killing them with kindness is taking way too long.

I have Xylophataquieopiaphobia, which is the fear of not pronouncing words correctly.

My wife said she wanted to try and get rid of her love handles.

I said she'd look stupid without any ears.

There was a fire at the tax department building in the city today.

It took six units three hours to get it out of control.

Never play with yourself right before you have sex.

Trust me; I learnt that the soft way.

My mum used to tell me if you can't say something nice, you probably have a lisp.

I can still enjoy sex at 55.
I live at 57, so it's only next door.

I bought a new 'Kings of Leon' smoke alarm.

Instead of beeping it goes,
"Whooooohhhhooooooa, your house is on fire."

Teenagers today drink twice as much as they did ten years ago.

To be fair, though, ten years ago they were only about five years old.

Give a man a fish and he'll eat for a day. Teach a man to fish and you've saved yourself a fish.

I wear a stethoscope so that in a medical emergency I can teach people a valuable lesson about assumptions.

I'm not saying that we should kill all the stupid people.

Just that we remove all the warning labels and let nature take its course.

Just because a screenplay is adapted doesn't mean we love it any less.

The world's best darts player has died. The cause of death was the world's worst darts player.

Some of the regulars here at the gym are a bit over developed.

Here's a tip, if your neck's as wide as your head, take a day off.

I used to work at a movie theatre.
One day I was on a ladder putting up a cinema poster.

A lady said, "Is King Kong coming?" I said, "No it's just the paste off my brush".

My pet mouse, Elvis, died today.
He was caught in a trap.

---

eBay is crap. I tried to look up cigarette lighters and all I got was 14,983 matches.

Telling people you're an 'old soul' is a great way to let people know you're deep but also super annoying.

That woman's bikini was so tight, I could hardly breathe.

Have you noticed that all the people in favour of birth control are already born?

Everyone's obsessed with eating right.
I just bought my kid a low G.I. Joe.

There's a new high tech fridge that will tell you if you've run out of something.
This eliminates the huge inconvenience of opening the door.

The guy who invented the fold out bed died.
He would have died in his sleep but the metal bar was digging into his back.

Few people remember Stevie's brother, "One-Hit" Wonder.

Methane's destroying our atmosphere so experts are trying to cut cow flatulence.
Clearly we need to ignore them when they say "Pull my hoof".

About a month before he died, we put greasy sunscreen all over my grandfather's back.

After that he went downhill very quickly.

If my wife ever turned into a zombie, I would not hesitate to wear a condom.

Apparently global warming could have saved the Titanic because that iceberg might not have been there. Damned humanity. We learn too late.

I'm going to be in this year's Moomba parade. I'll be on the Nexium float dressed as reflux.

My wife said she's had enough of my *Star Wars* 'bullshit' and wants to end our marriage.

Divorce is strong in this one.

Does your gay friend know that you call him your gay friend?

Doctors Without Borders does great work in Africa.

Doctors Without Degrees does incredible work in Chinatown.

The average time it takes for an elderly woman to get her ringing mobile phone out of her purse is 11 days.

The range of emotions a lobster feels from being chosen at the tank to being boiled alive must be how it feels to be drafted by Brisbane.

Our local church is asking for donations to buy a giant fundraising thermometer.

I found a wallet. If your VISA card is 4678 2345 2828 9001 exp. 11/17 CVV 810 call me as I've also got your I.D., license and business cards.

There's an app on my phone that makes me look fat. It's called "Camera".

I've nearly completed my year's resolution
of not saying or writing the word "poof" ...
Damn.

I just got skylights put in my place.
The woman upstairs is furious.

If you play guitar and harmonica at the
same time like Dylan you're a genius.

But strap some cymbals to your knees too
and you're an outcast.

I hate it when someone unexpectedly
comes in the room and you slam your
computer monitor down thinking that
you're on a laptop.

I've been watching paint dry all day,
but then some annoying bastard came
in and put the cricket on.

My wife and I like to dress up as
Adrian Balboa and Apollo Creed.

I think we're going through a Rocky patch.

I can't believe Coles called the cops on me for taking a few of their plastic bags.

Although they were filled with shopping at the time.

My wife asked me why I waste my time watching TV.

She thinks I should go find a job so we can get the power turned back on.

After some harsh words, there we were last night outside the pub, two guys against twenty.

Boy we kicked the shit out of those two guys.

Need an ark? I Noah guy.

I have a contact lens problem.
I have no contact lens solution.

We finally know what the Beach Boys song "Kokomo" is about.

It's all the places Donald Trump has bank accounts.

Just after I got home last night my neighbour came to my door.

He said, "You've left your lights on".

I said, "Without them I can't see my way around the house".

"Tsunami" is not in my phone's text dictionary. So if you ever get a text from me saying, "Trumang!" get the hell off the beach.

There are two types of people I hate:

1) People who find a way of putting animals into words that aren't actually there.

2) And hippocrites.

My bank just called me about suspicious activity on my account.

They didn't believe I bought a gym membership.

I'm cooking and I've just reached a new culinary milestone. I actually set off the neighbours' smoke alarm.

The first thing I look for in a woman is intelligence. Because if she doesn't have that, then there's a good chance she'll go out with me.

I remember a girl at school nicknamed "thunder thighs".

Her legs weren't fat though, they were blown off when she was struck by lightning.

I left my phone at home. I went home at lunch to grab it and saw my wife had sent me a text: "You've left your phone in the kitchen". Sigh ...

I've just spilled a bottle of carpet cleaner on the carpet. Now what?

You often hear "I'm not racist, but ..." but never the other way around. Like, "I'm racist, but the Asian guy next door is a frickin' legend".

I rang the Aussie Cricket team rooms yesterday. "Can I speak to our opening batsmen?"

A guy said "Sorry, they've just gone in to bat". I said, "I'll hold".

After seeing the movie, my wife is leaving me because I think I'm a Transformer.

I said, "I can change".
She said, "There you go again".

How many dance instructors does it take to change a light bulb?

Five ... Six ... Seven ... Eight ...

From now on I've decided to write all my jokes in capitals. This one was written in Canberra.

The furniture store keeps calling me even though I told them all I wanted was one night stand.

I've finished my Christmas cards early this year.

My Visa and American Express are both maxed out.

You can tell the gender of an ant by throwing it in water.

If it sinks — girl ant.
If it floats — buoyant.

Now Melania Trump can call herself the First Lady instead of the third wife.

I'm not a handsome man. On Halloween I went to tell the neighbours to turn their TV down and they gave me some lollies.

My Grandad drank a lot.
We called him alcopops.

Star Wars fan? If you think Han Solo is cool
you should meet his brother, Guitar.

My girlfriend told me I don't need to
use condoms anymore, which was
an interesting way to tell me she was
moving out.

My wife asked, "Why is it when things go
wrong, you always blame someone else?"

I said, "No, you're thinking of Dave, he's the
guy who blames other people".

I'm going to get a tattoo of a motorcycle
on my arse.

It'll explain the skid marks in my pants.

I wonder if it's rude for deaf people to talk
with food in their hands.

You know your kid loves you if they wouldn't unplug your life support to charge their phone.

People said I'd never get over my obsession with Phil Collins. But take a look at me now.

I wanted to be something really scary for Halloween this year so I dressed up as a phone battery at 2%.

They should put a picture of Donald Trump on every product that has nuts in it.

I wish I had a pair of skinny genes.

Mushroom flavoured Weetbix. The breakfast of champignons.

What's the difference between red and green?

Apparently bugger all if you're a cyclist.

At the zoo they had a baguette in a cage.

The zoo keeper told me it was bread
in captivity.

On our holiday I had one of those
'fish pedicures'. Those piranhas don't
muck around.

My motto is "Never say never".

Which makes it very difficult to tell people
my motto.

Friends, we need to prepare ourselves
for the day when Justin Bieber is doing
advertorials.

After spending twenty minutes trying to get
my wife's bra off, I've decided to give up.

I wish I'd never put it on now.

Dear Clive Palmer,

Thanks for auditioning for our new quiz show but we feel you may have misheard the title.

The show is actually called "Fact hunt".

I hired a handyman today and gave him a list of things to do. When I got home he'd only done tasks 1, 3, and 5. Turns out he only does odd jobs.

I complained to FedEx and they responded with a letter of apology.

Well, they sent it to my next door neighbour but he brought it over.

If you've never rewound a cassette tape with your finger, you have no right to complain about your slow Wi-Fi.

I made a voodoo doll of myself then gave it a lovely little back rub.

I'm proud of my daughter.
She has an anti-bullying wrist band.

She took it off a fat ginger kid.

When I was young I remember my parents
saying they wanted another kid.

I said, "I'd love a brother!"

They said, "That's not what we meant".

What do you call a Scotsman with
diarrhoea?

Bravefart.

My dog can find anything.
It's a Labragoogle.

I'm sure there's a bouncy castle inside our
local mosque. Every time I go past there's
always a load of shoes outside.

I just passed a man who's parked his car for
a sleep in a ditch by the side of the road.

Although I don't know how he can sleep
with his horn blaring.

Masseuse: How much pressure do you like?

Me: A lot.

Masseuse: Ok. With your huge mortgage, if the gigs dry up you'll have to sell the house.

Life is like a box of chocolates.
It doesn't last long if you're fat.

I told my daughter that there are two words in life that will open a lot of doors. Push and pull.

"You're such a little bitch, I'll bet you ride side-saddle" laughed the Lone Ranger's first sidekick, Taunt-O.

A recent study has found that women who carry a little extra weight live longer than the men who mention it.

You can tell I'm drunk by the number of made-up words I concoctulate.

I dated one girl for a while till we broke up.
But it was a mutual decision.

Both her and her husband thought I should go.

My wife and I have decided we don't want children.

If anybody does, we can drop them off tomorrow.

My poor knowledge of Greek mythology has always been my Achilles elbow.

When a woman says, "We need to talk", why is it never about football?

I told my boss I wanted a pay rise because three other companies were after me.

He said, "Which ones?"

I said, "The electric, gas and water".

Apple have abandoned plans to build ocean cruise liners after their prototype "The iTanic" kept syncing whenever it docked.

I've just changed my Wi-Fi broadband provider. From the Johnsons at number 85 to the Wilsons at number 89.

Scared the postman today by going to the door naked. I'm not sure what scared him more, my naked body or the fact that I knew where he lived.

Mate, that's not a photocopier, that's a shredder and look what you've done to your arse.

I told my wife she drew her eyebrows on too high. She looked surprised.

"Flat tyre?"

"Yeah."

"What happened?"

"Ran over a bottle."

"Didn't see it?"

"Damn kid had it under his coat."

My wife went to see a plastic surgeon but got confused and went to a tree surgeon instead.

Mind you, she does have a very nice bush now.

My dog's name is Minton and today he ate a shuttlecock. Bad Minton!

Boss: Stop copying and pasting your responses from old emails.

Me: No problem. Sent from my iPhone
Sent from my iPhone

Donald Trump has been saved by bodyguards after a man rushed him. The guards said the man was disturbed, but they had to protect him anyway.

I backed three horses today; Sunshine, Moonlight and Good Times. They all lost.

I blame it on the bookie.

Dear Life,

Please start using lubricant.

Thanks, Marty

I saw an ad in a shop window saying:
50" TV for sale, $30, volume stuck on full.

I thought "Well, I can't turn that down".

There's a chill in the air tonight so the whole family is gathered around a roaring Samsung Galaxy Note 7.

I always carry a picture of my wife and children in my wallet.

It reminds me why there's no money in there.

What do you call a fly with no wings?

Still a fly. The irony is unfortunate, but the name doesn't change. Sorry.

Reasons to get out of bed this morning:

1.

2.

3.

4.

5.

6.

7.

8. Full bladder.

That's all I've got.

Jeez it was warm yesterday. I stripped naked and opened all of the windows.

Oh boy, the taxi driver had the shits.

Any sandwich is a panini if you sit on it.

In Albert Park, if someone is "as big as a house", they're small and cramped with no car space.

The Somali Olympic Team has apologised after realising that shooting and sailing were two separate events.

My aunt's star sign was Cancer, so I guess it was predictable how she died.

She was attacked by a giant crab.

Everyone picks their nose. It's what you do with what you find up there that defines you as a person.

Wine tasting sounds so much more sophisticated than getting shitfaced.

My wife just fainted on the Melbourne Star Ferris wheel. But it's okay, she's slowly coming around.

Police have found a dead body at a Dominos which was covered in ham, cheese and pineapple. Friends said he may have topped himself.

I read a book about Stockholm Syndrome.
It was pretty bad at first, but by the end I
quite liked it.

———————————

I thought you might like this one: 1

———————————

What's the difference between a chick pea
and a lentil?

I've never had a lentil on me.

———————————

President Donald Trump is paid about
$50,000 a week which after tax is about
$50,000 a week.

———————————

A guy just tried to wash my windshield.
At first I ignored him, but after a few k's
I pulled over and asked him to get off my
bonnet.

———————————

Marriage teaches you love, patience,
forgiveness, compromise and a ton
of other shit you wouldn't need if you
were single.

———————————

Am I the only one that thought when Bugs Bunny dressed as a woman he was hot?

I've just bought a house with period features. My wife really hates that nickname.

I bet all those girls that ignored me in high school would still be pretty pleased with that decision.

I don't want to sound big headed but I wear a size XXL hat.

When my in-laws fight, my wife thinks I should leave the room instead of sitting there and scoring each round.

"You the bomb!" "No you the bomb!"

A compliment in Australia.
An argument in the Middle East.

My mate John's sex change operation went very well. They did such a good job he's still trying to reverse out of the hospital car park.

_____

They say if you lose one sense the other senses are enhanced. That's why folk with no sense of humour have a bigger sense of self-importance.

_____

Operator: "Triple 0. What's your emergency?"

Me: (Sounds of struggle) "Hi. I offered this emu my sandwich but I changed my mind."

_____

Welcome to Rambler's Club. The 1st rule of Ramblers Club, well it wasn't actually the 1st rule we came up with as we had other rules but we had a bit of a think about what order we should put them in and Barry thought it might be an idea to put them in the ...

_____

"$20 on grey." — Colour-blind guy playing roulette.

_____

I saw a sign in the window of the TAB saying 'Open Sunday 10-1'.

I'll have $50 on that. They were open last Sunday.

When I see lovers names carved into a tree I don't think it's cute, I just think it's strange how many people take knives on a date.

I've become addicted to drinking brake fluid.

My doctor's worried but I can stop any time.

Horses sleep standing up. As does anyone stuck talking to my cousin at a party.

Welcome to Thesaurus Club. The first rule of Thesaurus Club is you don't talk, converse, discuss, speak, chat, deliberate, confer, gossip ...

My wife asked me to pass her the lip balm but I accidentally gave her some superglue instead. She's still not talking to me.

There's a gang going though Myer stores, systematically shoplifting clothes in order of size.

The police believe they're still at large.

Welcome to Latecomers Club ...
(crickets chirp) ...

Sigh ...

Roadworks are like Visa.
It's everywhere you want to be.

Music was better when ugly people were allowed to make it.

I asked my wife, "Would you still love me if I was ugly and fat?"

She said, "Yes I do".

A radio announcer in France was arrested for defending terrorists.

I think he's one of those "Shock Jacques".

I used to date a dyslexic girl. Weird girl.
I took her home and she cooked my sock.

You know that feeling when you're craving a Krabby Patty so bad but the Krusty Krab is closed ... and also fictional.

I think ceiling fans are really just helicopters who gave up on their dreams and opted for an office job.

I've started a new workout routine.
Every day I do 20 diddly-squats.

The doctor said I needed to stop drinking and smoking immediately!

The rules in his waiting room are tough.

To save time, my psychiatrist just throws bananas, crackers and nuts on his desk and asks me to point at what I am.

My pain in the arse neighbour was banging on my door at three o'clock this morning.

Luckily I was still up practising my drums.

Women only say that I'm ugly until they find out how much money I make.

Then they say that I'm ugly and poor.

If you're skydiving and your parachute doesn't open, don't stress.

You have the rest of your life to fix it.

Do you think Charles Schulz's wife used to show him her vagina and then pull it away at the last second?

The holes in crocs shoes are for where your dignity leaks out.

If you need a gun I know a guy called T-Rex. He's a small arms dealer.

Your potato salad recipe is not a "family secret".

Your uncle Bob who cooks crystal meth in his caravan is a family secret.

I can explain the first rule of Patronising Club to you if you want, although it's pretty complicated.

This morning I was woken with a blowjob.

I need to start sleeping with my mouth closed.

Remind me, if I'm ever in hospital, make sure I'm never surrounded by my friends and family.

It usually doesn't end well.

I woke up really upset this morning when I realised it was 9-11 because I was supposed to be at work at 8.30.

I was in Myer today and I splashed out on some new underwear so they made me buy them.

The sat nav in my new car uses Bono's voice but it's not that good.

The streets have no name and I still haven't found what I'm looking for.

How do I turn off the autocorrect function on my wife?

What's Batman's favourite fruit?

BA-NA-NA-NA-NA-NA-NA-NA-BA-NA-NA-NA-NA-NA-NA-NA

Grapefruit.

When I'm mad at my wife I just wash her jeans then put them in the dryer on hot then put them in her drawer.

Welcome to uncertainty club?

My wife told me to get our red headed son ready for school.

So I beat him up and took his lunch money.

People are worried about the effects of genetically modified crops but "there's no proof of any adverse effects" said a carrot.

Our neighbours have changed the name of their Wi-Fi network to WeCanHearYouHavingSex.

My ex-wife says it was my obsession with horoscopes that Taurus apart.

I forgot to bring mum her lunch so she started eating the sofa.

But then again, she's always had a suite tooth.

Now my wife wants to leave me because she says I love football more than her.

I'm very upset. We've been together for ten seasons.

I just replaced our bed with a trampoline.
My wife hit the roof.

My wife said, "Did you know butterflies
only live for two days?"

I said, "I think that's a myth".

She said, "No, I'm pretty sure it's a
butterfly".

I bought my daughter a power fan for her
birthday. She was blown away.

I just bought some coconut shampoo.
I don't know why, though. I don't own
a coconut.

My wife broke up with me because of my
gambling. All I can think of is how to win
her back.

If you see someone buy an ice cream,
a drink and popcorn at the movies,
they're a drug dealer.

There's no other explanation for that
sort of income.

Animal Fact: Baby frogs are called tadpoles but teenage frogs are called petulant pains in the arse.

My dog only responds to commands in Spanish.

He's Espanyol.

How to cook the perfect amount of pasta:

1. Pour how much pasta you think you need into a pot.

2. Wrong.

My wife said to me, "You treat our relationship like some kind of game!" which unfortunately cost her 5 points and a penalty chance.

According to the National Retailers Association, the top two most shop-lifted items are DVDs and panties. That gives a whole new meaning to the term 'box set'.

Boobs are like the sun. Taking a quick look is fine, but staring isn't.

I guess that's what sunglasses are for.

My wife texted me: Wanna come home at lunchtime for a quickie?

I texted back: It's pronounced 'Quiche'.

My dog's just blown his kennel up.
Bloody Yorkshire Terrorist.

Today I met a microbiologist.
He was bigger than I imagined.

I was at "Not Quite Right" Pets. I bought a faulty cat that only had five lives.

Midwife for sale.

Can deliver.

The Salvos are trying to count the number of homeless people around Crown Casino but admit, "We really don't have a system". Coincidentally, that's the same reason people are homeless around Crown Casino.

———————

Pirate: The cannons be ready, captain.

Captain: Are.

———————

I've got mood poisoning.

Must be something I hate.

———————

Scientology is like a warm bed on a cold day. Tough to get out of and not surprising that Tom Cruise and John Travolta are in it together.

———————

My dog always sniffs the same post on our walks. Apparently it's like a message board for neighbourhood dogs. I think he's checking his P-mail. "You've got P".

———————

Remember Pat Cash? The best thing about being married to him would be if he got kidnapped and you paid the ransom quick enough you get cash back.

There are a lot of Adelaide jokes, but people from Adelaide have a great sense of humour.

They have to, they're from Adelaide.

Geometry is hard. I tried to quickly draw a square but I ended up with an octagon.

That's what happens when you cut corners.

"Knock knock."

"Who's there?"

"Dejav."

"Dejav who?"

"Knock knock."

I was in my car today, when I saw a Chinese woman driving with her hazard lights on.

I thought to myself, "At least she's honest".

———————————

I rang a phone sex line. The hot girl on the other end said, "Hey sexy, what can I do for you?"

I said, "Call me back, it's cheaper".

———————————

BOOM

Wife: "What was that?"

Me: "My shirt fell on the ground."

Wife: "It sounded a lot heavier than that."

Me: "I was in it."

———————————

Hey vegetarians.
My food shits on your food.

———————————

PMS = Prepare to Meet Satan.

———————————

Billion dollar idea: An app that sends you a text when the traffic light turns green.

———————————

A bunch of scumbags stole 20 crates of Red Bull from a supermarket yesterday.

I don't know how the bastards sleep at night.

I love digital cameras because they allow you to reminisce immediately.

"Look at us there. So young. Where do the seconds go?"

The most common surname in China is Chang, correct me if you think it's Wong.

What's got no teeth and smells?

The gearbox in my wife's car.

I'm on the snake diet. It's the one where you lie on the floor all day, eat 25% of your body weight, and hiss at anyone who comes near you.

"I can't go to a party without getting completely smashed."
– Greek dinner plate.

I pawned my chess set, which was ironic.

———————————

Some mornings I wake up angry.
Other mornings I just let her sleep.

———————————

The Mexicans are pretty pissed off about Trump's wall. But they'll get over it.

———————————

A terrorist attack has blown away two local houses, one made of straw and the other made of wood. Police think that it's probably a lone wolf.

———————————

My problem is I have just enough money to get into trouble tonight but not enough money to make bail.

———————————

They're closing the movie theatre complex at Chadstone and the snack bar is having a sale.

They've gone crazy. Some prices are nearly down to retail!

———————————

Just so we're clear, I am not responsible for what my face does when you talk.

———————————

"Doctor, I've hurt my penis in a surfing accident."

"Hit the board when you wiped out?"

"No I slammed my laptop shut when my wife walked in."

———————————

"What if I tried to put a ball somewhere and you tried to stop me?"
— The guy that invented sport.

———————————

I went to an Indian restaurant last night and tried a pelican curry.

Food was ok, but the bill was enormous.

———————————

I jumped into the bay with my friends today, even though I didn't want to.

Stupid pier pressure.

———————————

A photon goes through airport security and is asked if it has any luggage.

The photon says, "No, I'm travelling light".

Why should men never wear Ukrainian underpants?

Because Chernobyl fall out.

How many Germans does it take to screw in a light bulb?

One.

They're efficient and not very funny.

Last Xmas I said to my wife, "I bet you can wrap presents with your eyes shut".

She said, "I probably could".

I said, "Great, I'll just go and get yours".

Marriage is the process of finding out what kind of man your wife would have preferred.

I gave my seat to a blind man on the bus.

Lost my job as a bus driver.

I'm starting to think that I'll never have a monkey apprentice.

Why was the snowman looking through a bag of carrots?

He was picking his nose.

Always leave "Get Well Soon Cards" on the mantel. If you have unexpected guests they'll think you've been too sick to clean the house.

I answered the door today and a 6ft beetle punched me in the face then called me fat and ugly.

Apparently there's a nasty bug going round.

Apply for a job at the Deed Poll office if you want to make a name for yourself.

A bloke on a tractor just drove past me shouting "The end of the world is coming!"

I think it was Farmer Geddon.

I had a German girlfriend who hated it when I pulled her hair during sex.

She said it made her armpits sore.

Relationships are a lot like algebra. You look at your X and wonder Y.

I'm old enough to remember when there was only one fat kid in class photos.

I'm not concerned with babies on airplanes, but grown adults who don't fly often need their own terminal.

When you go to jail, they take away your shoelaces so you don't kill yourself.
I haven't got the slightest idea how you'd kill yourself with shoelaces. You'd have to be the MacGyver of killing yourself.

It seems like no matter how much mascara I put on my penis, I can't seem to make it thicker, fuller or longer lasting.

My wife made me promise not to make any more jokes about her weight.

Ok, but she really needs to lighten up.

[Enter Password]

Wrong

Wrong

Wrong

[Reset Password]

NEW PASSWORD CANNOT BE OLD PASSWORD

Seriously?

I never dreamed that one day I'd become a grumpy old man.

And yet here I am, killing it!

I'm having car problems. Those warning lights on the dash come on a lot. Yesterday I saw the "check oil" light. Then the "Check engine" light came on. I couldn't check the engine, there was too much smoke. Then the "game over" light came on. That was a new one.

———————————

Help colleagues see "the bigger picture" by printing on A3.

———————————

Genie: What's your first wish?

Dave: I wish I was rich.

Genie: Granted, what's your second wish?

Rich: I want lots of money.

———————————

The guy who bullied me at school still takes my lunch money.

But on the upside, he makes a great Subway footlong.

———————————

For a while I used to live in a big tractor tyre, but it got a puncture so now I just live in a flat.

———————————

I just bought some Jamie Oliver sausages at Woolies. On the pack it says "prick with a fork".

Can't really argue with that.

————————

I've just noticed my wife's wearing her sexy underwear. And I know what that means.

She's behind with her washing.

————————

The only place success comes before work is in the dictionary.

But keep in mind success still comes after 'bribery' and 'sexual favours'.

————————

Steve Buscemi is what would happen if a foot could sneeze.

————————

My daughter bet me I couldn't do a butterfly impression.

I thought to myself, that's got to be worth a flutter.

————————

I hate people that don't understand football but still go along to games to deliberately cause trouble and ruin it for everybody else! Bloody umpires.

I'm trying to explain my car trouble to the mechanic without resorting to sound effects. Nup.

My wife said she's leaving me because I can't do anything right when it comes to housework.

I'm upset. It took me ages to mop the carpet.

I won't be going to the Logies again. The invitation said "Black tie only" but when I got there I noticed that other people wore shirts and pants too.

Don't you hate people who don't know the difference between "your" and "you're."

There so stupid.

You know what they say about cliffhangers ...

I sleep better naked. Why can't this flight attendant understand that?

Arguing with a woman is like reading a software license agreement.

In the end you ignore it all, wait for the end and click "I agree".

A recent survey indicates the Smartphone is now the number one hand held device pushing the penis down to second spot.

Is it too late to start calling shampoo "hair soap?"

Whenever I go out lately, I'm always followed by a bird with long legs and skinny beak.

I think I'm being storked.

When I was younger I didn't know what good tits even looked like, but I knew that one day I'd come across them.

My mate has no hands.

I feel for him.

My wife left a note on the TV today saying "It's just not working. I'm leaving".

I turned it on, and there's nothing wrong with it! Stupid woman.

Why do Avon ladies walk funny?

Their lipstick.

My wife told me that our son feels neglected.

Wow, we have a son?

I used to have a job at the zoo circumcising elephants.

The money wasn't great, but the tips were huge.

I got an email.

"Your ex-girlfriend has endorsed you on LinkedIn for 'Ignoring Glaring Personal Issues!'"

A blind guy walks into a bar.
And a table. And a chair ...

Gambling has brought our family together.

We had to move to a smaller house.

I just slipped on the floor of the local library. I was in the non-friction section.

What stands in a paddock and goes "Oooooh!"?

A cow with no lips.

My friend David is a victim of ID theft.

Now we just call him 'Dav'.

Head and Shoulders shampoo should make a body wash called Knees and Toes.

Some guy just threw dough, cheese, salami and tomatoes in my face.

I said, "You wanna pizza me?"

A Nigerian Prince has died and left his millions to a cat. He tried to give away his fortune for years, but no one ever responded to his emails.

I wonder how the guy who made the first clock knew what time it was?

In my glove box I collect parking tickets because they're like shares.

The longer you keep them, the more they're worth.

Kanye West is said to be recovering well in hospital after a nine hour operation to remove his head from his arsehole.

They've just released a perfume made from holy water. They've called it Eau my God.

I'm gonna stop being so pessimistic.
It's never gonna work out.

I just sold some homing pigeons on
eBay for the 28th time.

Sex education classes in school should just
be listening to a baby crying for six hours
straight while watching the same cartoon
on repeat.

Why do they call it a building? It looks like
they're finished. Why isn't it a "built"?

If you ever feel like your job is meaningless
just remember it's someone's job to fit
indicators to BMWs.

Last night somehow I swallowed
some Lego.

The doctors aren't too worried,
but I'm shitting bricks.

INTERVIEW TIP: When asked if you have any questions, try not to say "What makes you think you're getting out of this room alive?"

What do you call someone who points out the obvious?

Someone who points out the obvious.

If you're offered a sales job at a farm, it will be largely field-based.

If anyone knows a good fish pun please let minnow.

You may be a pop/rock fan but telling your boss that you need a day off because your "Sex is on fire" will have limited success.

You're always told to "Stay safe. Wear something bright at night".

But the velcro on this hi-vis vest keeps getting caught on my doona.

The definition of irony: Not knowing the difference between a definition and an example.

Keep your guests on their toes by putting all their belongings on a high shelf.

I'm kind of glad dinosaurs are extinct because I'm pretty sure I'd try and ride one after I'd had a few drinks.

My limbo team and I go way back.

The only time incorrectly isn't spelled incorrectly is when it's spelled incorrectly.

Just want to thank my mailman for delivering my recycling directly to my house.

"I just went on a hike and suddenly I can tell everyone what's right and wrong."
— Moses

I go to the gym so infrequently that I still call it the James.

If you ever feel like life's passing by too fast, just get a hangover.

I just got mad at my daughter for farting on our leather couch while she was bare-assed naked and my anger was 100% based in jealousy.

Wind farms are ridiculous. As if this country doesn't have enough wind of its own without wasting electricity making more of it by running these big fans.

Just got sacked from my job as a dishwasher.

I kept putting the plates and bowls in the wrong order.

The boss said I'm dishlexic.

My younger brother was named after my father.

That's fine but it's a bit confusing when your brother's called Dad.

What's the difference between a candle and a curry?

A candle only burns at one end.

Hey mums washing kid's faces with spit? Cut that shit out.

For my birthday I got a universal remote control. I thought to myself, "This changes everything".

Last week I replaced every window in my house.

I realised this morning I had a crack in my glasses.

Doctors are telling us that smoking weed causes memory loss.

That's crap. Next they'll be telling us smoking weed causes memory loss.

_____

This week I'm going to record *The X Factor* and watch it an hour later.

That way I can fast forward through the shit and just watch the ads.

_____

Breaking news:

ne ws

_____

I hate it when women turn the light off before having sex.

It makes it really difficult for me to see them through the window.

_____

He's old. At his last birthday party, the candles cost more than the cake.

_____

I cabn tuype 300 wods s ninute.

_____

It's so cold this morning I had to plug my nose and bear down to get my penis to pop back out.

I bought a grand piano.
It was $1000.

Grandpa's advice: Never pick a fight with an ugly person. They've got nothing to lose.

I've been waiting here at the doctors for my mate to finish his prostate exam for three hours now.

Somebody needs to pull their finger out!

She's old. Her walking frame has an airbag.

I watched a girl at the gym this morning do three sets of selfies.

How many immature men does it take to screw in a light bulb?

Ha! Screw!

Operator: "Triple 0 what's your emergency?"

Me: "My kid just swallowed a lighter!"

Operator: "What's your address?"

Me: "Never mind, I found some matches."

Everyone keeps telling me I'm paranoid.

It's like a conspiracy or something.

I rang up work this morning.

"My neighbour died last night. I'm going to need some time off work."

They said, "Sorry for your loss. Take as much time off as you need".

I said, "Thank you. It'll be about eighteen years, with good behaviour".

The woman next to me on the roller coaster just wouldn't stop screaming!

It's like she'd never seen a penis before.

Do you think horses worry about unicorns like humans worry about aliens?

I'll always assume the worst when I see a dude smelling his finger.

If a girl doesn't smile back at me I assume she thinks it'd lead to sex so awesome that everything else she ever did would be disappointing.

When do you think witches will embrace modern technology and start riding vacuum cleaners?

My wife told me, "I always feel so self-conscious when we're out in public".

I laughed, "Don't worry, you aren't that ugly".

She said, "No, but you are".

Anything I have ever learned about One Direction, The Kardashians and Lara Bingle has been completely against my will.

I think landlords who don't allow dogs but DO allow children don't know very much about children.

I have a certain reticence, if reticence is the word, about the word reticence.

I was standing in front of the mirror when my wife walked in.

I said, "I'm bloody huge! Will you help me?"

She said, "Of course" and moved the mirror further away.

Facebook is a weapon of mass distraction.

Coming up next on The Apathetic Gameshow Network, a new episode of The Price is Alright.

It's nearly impossible to shop for women these days because human trafficking is illegal here.

Fire drills are useful because in the event of an actual fire, everyone would indeed walk calmly down the stairs making small talk.

It's true I flirt a lot but my wife is super cool with it along with a lot of other things she doesn't know about.

Say what you want about Streets Blue Ribbon Ice Cream, but it won, you guys, so have some goddamned respect.

"I don't think you understand me at all", she said accusingly in her thick Scottish accent.

I blink. I pause. I said, "Haggis bagpipes what?"

"Ask me no questions, I'll tell you no lies" is a good caveat, but not a great way to start a job interview.

I've already gained back ten of the five kilos I lost last summer.

Chocolate tastes different when you pretend a fat German kid drowned in it.

People who can fall asleep quickly freak me out. Don't they have thoughts?

Is it just me, or are there other people?

I always offer the delivery guy an extra $10 to hand-feed me the pizza.

Some people are as useless as the 'ay' in 'okay'.

My kid comes home from school and asks me questions. "Daddy, what's a light year?" "It's half the calories of a regular year."

I'm proud that not wearing a watch has never stopped me from looking at my wrist when people ask me what time it is.

I'm not sure about this AA meeting.
There's a three drink minimum.

Dad didn't want to send me to a catholic
school because the teachers hit the kids,
so he sent me to a high school, where the
kids hit the teachers.

It's a bird! It's a plane! It's ... Superman!
And he's ... pooping.

Nope, sorry, it's a bird.

I am easily the smartest and most
attractive person in this compulsive liars
support group.

Doctor Doctor!

Do you think your surname influenced your
choice of career?

The inventor of autocorrect went from zero
to hero in a matter of seconds.

My wife can no longer attend today's meeting of Double Entendre club.

Now I have to fill her slot.

I always got asked questions by the teacher that she knew I didn't know.

"Fields, what's a pronoun?"

"Um, a noun that gets paid?"

"No, what's a homonym?"

"Um, a gay nym?"

If you wash down vitamins with bourbon they still work, right?

Harry Potter Condoms: In case you need something for your wand while entering the chamber of secrets so you don't get hog warts.

If we go out to eat and you keep trying to talk to me after the food arrives I'll call the cops.

I watched a gang bang porno involving several bus drivers and one woman.

Nothing happened for an hour, then suddenly they all came at the same time.

I can't wait until time-machines were invented.

I just try to live my life in such a way that if it ever does flash before my eyes it will be worth watching.

Welcome to the 21st century where deleting your history has become more important than making it.

I went to Coles and swapped two boxes of raisins for one box of sultanas.

I can't believe the currant exchange rate.

"Dad, why's my sister called Paris?"

"Because that's where she was conceived."

"Thanks dad."

"No worries, Airline Toilet."

I've decided to marry a pencil. Can't wait to introduce my friends to my bride 2B.

When my blonde neighbour asked me if I knew about items missing from her clothesline I nearly shit her pants.

I'm going on a blind date tonight. I hope our Labradors get on.

Have fun at the playground in McDonald's tonight, single dads.

My daughter eats pizza upside-down so I asked her why and she said it was so the yummy part was on her tongue so where's her goddamn Nobel prize?

My recent google searches:

How to detangle my daughter's hair.

How to treat a really tough tangle.

How to cut out a tangle.

Hats.

On his deathbed my grandfather gave me some sound advice.

He said "It's worth spending money on good speakers".

I was at the chemist. I said, "I'm after some condoms".

He said, "Just a minute".

I said, "Yeah, that's them".

I remember my late father saying to me, "Sorry I'm late".

My wife is out of town and I'm a little lonely so tonight I'm going to pay a hooker to come over and fall asleep in a track suit on my couch at 8.30.

I love my alarm clock collection.
It's the reason I get up in the morning.

Volleyball is just a more intense version of "don't let the balloon touch the floor".

I remember asking my mother,
"Mum, am I ugly?"

She said, "I've told you not to call me mum in public".

My cousin drowned. At his funeral we laid a life jacket on his coffin.

It's what he would have wanted.

My deaf girlfriend was talking in her sleep last night. She nearly took my eye out.

I hope I never have to explain to a time travelling 9-year-old me why I spend more money on ties than roller coasters.

I got a new aftershave called "Breadcrumbs".

The birds love it.

The Invisible Man married the Invisible Woman. Their kids aren't much to look at either.

My wife says I'm spoken for.

Viagra eye drops make you look hard.

Welcome to this emergency meeting of the premature ejaculation society.

Thank you all for coming so quickly.

Tonight I'm going to watch a movie with my girlfriend.

Can anyone recommend a girlfriend?

SHORT JOKES FOR TALL PEOPLE

Wouldn't it be ironic if everyone went blind in the year 2020?

'Twas the night before Christmas,
and all through the house,

Not a creature was stirring,
not even a mouse.

I really should have invested in one of those carbon monoxide detectors.

People have always enjoyed working in Antiques Shops. Nothing new there.

A bloke goes into the doctor's. "Doc, I've got a cricket ball stuck up my backside."

The doctor says, "How's that?"

He says, "Don't you start".

I've just invented an invisibility cloak; anything under it is completely invisible.

I'm still working out the kinks though. You can still see the cloak itself.

I have a friend named Jay, but we call him J for short.

———————————

My wife said she was leaving me because I always exaggerate.

I was so shocked I nearly tripped over my dick.

———————————

It's impossible to eat a Toblerone in winter without injuring yourself.

———————————

My friend's dog is a cross between a pit bull and a collie. He rips your leg off then goes for help.

———————————

My dad never loved me as a child.

I can't blame him really.

I wasn't born until he was an adult.

———————————

When I dance I look like I'm carrying a boiling hot pot of soup with my bare hands and can't find a place to set it down.

———————————

I'm very loyal in a relationship, all relationships. When I'm with my mother, I don't look at other mums and think, "Mmmm. I wonder what her macaroni and cheese tastes like".

If the Olympics had rocking back and forth on the toilet to jar one loose I think I could medal.

Sydney University researchers said this week that the drug Naltrexone could be used to curb a kleptomaniac's impulse to steal. Although the drug is not covered by health funds, doctors say kleptomaniacs should have no problem obtaining it.

When I was a kid, we were so poor, when my cousin broke his arm we had to take him out to the airport for X-rays.

If Girth Brooks isn't already a porn star's name then somebody's not doing their job.

A dog goes into a hardware store and says, "I'd like a job please". The hardware store owner says, "We don't hire dogs. Why don't you go join the circus?" The dog replies, "What would the circus want with a plumber?"

I was telling a bloke, "My brother makes cars out of other cars. He put together the motor from a Ford, wheels from a Honda, and seats from a Mazda".

The bloke asked, "What'd he get?"

I said, "5 years".

I was driving and went through a red light. A cop pulled me over and asked, "Didn't you see that red light?"
I said, "Yes".
He said, "Why didn't you stop?"
I said, "Mate, if you've seen one you've seen them all".

Cannibals love Dominoes. Not for the pizza, but for the delivery guy.

Women who have a tattoo really turn me on. When I see a woman with a tattoo I think, "Now here's a girl who's comfortable making a decision she'll regret in the future".

When I was a child, there were times when we just had to entertain ourselves.

So we'd all gather in the living room and turn on the TV.

I like to play blackjack. I'm not addicted to gambling. I'm addicted to sitting in a semi-circle.

I met a soldier who was seriously injured in Afghanistan.

He's got a steel plate in his head and a prosthetic leg made from aluminium and titanium.

He's become both a friend and an alloy.

Give a man a jacket and he'll be warm for a day.

Teach a man to jacket and he'll never leave the house.

The popularity of origami has increased tenfold.

A Roman walks into a bar, holds up two fingers, and says, "Five beers, mate".

Last night my wife and I watched three DVDs back to back.

Luckily I was the one facing the TV.

Regular naps prevent old age. Especially if you take them while you're driving.

Since it started raining, all my daughter has done is look sadly through the window.

If it gets any worse, I'll have to let her in.

Ask not what your friends can do for you, but what you can do to make them feel guilty for not offering in the first place.

Justin Bieber getting tasered would be the most watched YouTube video of all time.

I never feel more racist than when trying to find my waiter at a Chinese restaurant.

I'd be more of a fan of exercising if calories screamed when you burned them.

Women are fascinated by mythical creatures like unicorns, vampires, and men who are good listeners.

If Leonardo da Vinci posted the Mona Lisa on Instagram today, it would get 30 likes, tops.

Breaking financial news, Winnie the Pooh creator AAA Milne has been downgraded to AA Milne.

Definitions

A WEEK OLD:

1. Something that has lasted seven days.

2. What Scottish people call a viral infection of the upper respiratory tract.

If a guide dog shits on the street, who picks it up?

Never get your photograph taken at a fancy dress party in case you get amnesia and it's the first piece of the puzzle you find.

My wife says she's leaving me because of my addiction to antidepressants.

Guess I won't be needing them anymore.

People who think I'm pretentious need to walk a mile in my Louis Vuitton soft suede slippers.

Hey, can the next one of you who travels back in time to kill Hitler stop on the way back and bring us 1971 Rod Stewart?

___

A woman walks up to me at the pool and said, "Your eyes match your swim trunks".

I said, "Are they bulging?"

___

Acting is tough. I auditioned for a Christmas play but "wasn't quite right" for the role as one of the three wise men.

___

I can text my bank a balance enquiry and they text me back with my balance.

It's a cool feature but I didn't think the 'LOL' was necessary.

___

My mum always told me to put on clean underwear "in case I was involved in an accident".

Pointless advice. By the time the car finished rolling, I'd already shit myself.

___

I just replaced my shoelaces with earphones.

Now they tie themselves.

When I can't sleep I try counting sheep, but my ADHD is a nightmare.

One sheep, two sheep, dog, pig, old McDonald, Hey Macarena!

I've been in India for a week and I still haven't seen the sun rise in the morning.

And unless it comes up out of the toilet bowl, I probably never will.

Turn and look at the person on your left. Now look at the person on your right.

Both of those people now think you're kind of creepy.

Any of you guys want a dog that can fart Ritchie Blackmore's entire guitar riff from "Smoke on the Water"?

What's red and bad for your teeth?

A brick.

My daughter asked me to make her a ballerina's costume.

I had no idea where to start, but then I put tu and tu together.

Jeep are giving away $500 worth of fuel with every new car ordered this week.

So it should only take another few bucks to fill the tank.

For those using dating sites, please be advised that GSOH does not mean "Great Set Of Hooters".

What's so great about being "stable" and "well adjusted" anyway?

Valets don't just like parking a little, they like parking lots.

My wife reading the eulogy: "We are gathered here today because SOMEBODY (glares at coffin) couldn't stay alive".

When the titanic is spoken about, no one ever mentions the 1000 miles of trouble free luxury cruising before the iceberg ...

If dentists make money from people with unhealthy teeth, why should I trust a toothbrush that 9 out of 10 dentists recommend?

Don't judge me. What I do in public is my own damn business.

Dolly Parton didn't retire, she's just been at a mammogram appointment since 1987.

If you were 7 years old when that cover of 'Red Red Wine' was released, UB40 now.

I need to lose weight so I've been doing some serious thinking about cutting down from cakes to cupcakes.

There's no stronger bond than the one between a parent and their liquor cabinet.

Americans say they need to arm themselves to protect themselves.

They're serious, too. Just recently an American dentist had to fly 4,000 miles to protect himself from an elderly African lion.

"I watched a show about little green men last night."

"Aliens?"

"No, Smurfs. My TV's buggered."

Everything I know about opera I learned from Bugs Bunny when he was a barber.

I got an email about processed meat causing cancer but I think it's just spam.

It's all fun and games until Grandpa has a flashback during Battleship.

"You're Listening to Jewish radio, Tel Aviv, 1422 on the dial. But for you, 1250."

I bought her a new book called Cheap and Easy Vegetarian Cooking. Which was perfect for her because not only was she a vegetarian ...

My father was dyslexic.

Luckily it's not geometric.

My wife and I were having sex. Half way through she got up and told me she's leaving me for the guy next door. Then he came in and gave me a blow job.

Have you noticed since everyone has a phone camera these days nobody talks about seeing UFOs like they used to?

You can't judge a book by its cover, but if the cover says The A-Z Of Accountancy, you get a pretty good idea.

———————————

My wife suffers in silence louder than any person I know.

———————————

I got interrupted downloading the new version of iTunes by a pop up that asked if I wanted to download an even newer version of iTunes.

———————————

I always knew I had something special that attracts women towards other men.

———————————

Looking back now, it was probably a mistake to join Hindsight Club.

———————————

There's something new to help people who don't know how to change lanes.

It's called Public Transport.

———————————

The motto of $2 shops must be "Customers should feel like they're visiting their old Auntie and discovering she's a hoarder".

You'd think the inevitable 5 minutes deleting Out-Of-Office replies would deter people from even looking at the Reply-All button, but no ...

Friend: "I just blew a speaker in my car."

Me: "What kind?"

Friend: "Motivational."

Calvin Klein has a cunning plan to make us buy more underwear.

I saw the price of his boxers and shit myself.

I wish I knew how to use "as it were" correctly.

I get so jealous when I hear people say it, as it were.

Sorry I drank your warning shots.

I just missed my Jetstar check-in this morning by one minute and had to spend $400 to get the next flight. Most expensive one minute of my life, apart from the conception of our daughter.

I wonder if other dogs think poodles are members of a weird religious cult.

I clicked my torch on and off out my bedroom window.

.just.learned.morse.code.anyone.want. to.chat

And in the dark distance I saw

shut.the.hell.up.

New Zealanders are moving to Australia more than ever right now.

They've heard there's no jobs here.

Just curious. How long after walking into someone's house for a dinner party is it acceptable to ask for their Wi-Fi password?

I booked a holiday. Seven nights in Coolangatta. I said to the travel agent, "What do I do during the days?" He said, "I don't care but keep the hell out of Coolangatta".

It's hard to tell a chemistry joke nowadays because all the good ones argon.

A guy used the word 'ain't' to me today.

It's apparently a contraction of two words.

But which ones?

I own the tallest horse in town.
It's really high.

When I sit on it I understand what it's like to be a vegan.

This job I've got at the shoe recycling plant is sole destroying.

If you could see all the other people who drank at a water fountain before you, no one would ever drink at a water fountain.

Life is too short to remove a USB safely.

"Be strong" I whispered to my Wi-Fi signal.

I've noticed lots of people are named after where they were conceived.

For example Sydney or London.

I must tell my friend, Ally.

My footsteps are 1 million times louder when I'm sneaking.

If I ever get married again I want my last name to be hyphenated.

Mr. and Mrs. Hyphenated.

Well the house is all clean but the party's not until tomorrow so my wife says we're going to have to find someplace else to live tonight.

———————————

The cops arrested me for stealing a sign that said "and Emergency".

I told them I found it by Accident.

———————————

They'll continue to make Fast & Furious movies until it's a bunch of old men trying to get out of a supermarket car park.

———————————

I'd be drunk already but I overslept.

———————————

Scars are tattoos with better back-stories.

———————————

I've just been banned from the driving-range for life.

I think they should make it clearer that it's for golf.

———————————

Most expensive sight gag ever:

"Why did you build a mountain
in your paddock?"

"For the cattle."

"Why?"

"It's great for their calves."

Clothes maketh the man.

But usually a child maketh the clothes.

I saved time doing gardening by renaming
the weeds "plants".

You've heard of alphabet soup? Now get
ready for Times New Ramen.

My mate told me, "There's a guy in my
street who's got his Christmas decorations
up already".

I said, "That's nothing, the old woman next
door to me hasn't taken hers down from
last year. And they're making her house
smell funny".

I was chatting to this woman.

She said, "So tell me, what do they call you?"

I said, "They call me Tripod".

She said, "Oooh. Well hung, huh?"

I said, "No. I'm a bit odd and I smell like tripe".

If the movie theatre slightly lowered their prices I wouldn't have to tape chocolate bars around my kid's torso like a suicide bomber.

I just got kicked out of Best & Less for having my bottom teeth.

My neighbour was horribly disfigured in a car crash.

So I knocked on her door and told her to start closing her bedroom curtains.

"Open mic poetry starts in five minutes" works better than "Last drinks".

I get the impression that, if they could, cats would correct your grammar.

_____

Don't waste my time.

That's my job.

_____

Beauty is in the eye of the:

A) Holder

B) Holder

C) Holder

D) Holder

_____

"Can you help me, Doctor? I seem to have lost my sense of direction."

"So it seems," said the butcher.

_____

I'm not sure why but the bigger the sunglasses, the bigger the bitch.

_____

My 20-year-old daughter called me.

"Dad? Um, John and I have been together for a while now, and we were wondering if you wouldn't mind coming over and baby-proofing our flat?"

I said, "Of course my princess."

So I went round and cut off his dick.

At what point in life when you want to do something do you go from being "old enough" to "young enough"?

I went for an interview as a Vet.

The guy said, "Do you have any experience treating animals?"

I said, "Absolutely. My dog goes through 10 packets of Schmackos a week".

It's so sad that birthday cakes don't live long enough to have birthdays of their own.

"You know what I'm going to ask
you when you walk in the door today
don't you?"

... And other texts that make husbands
nervous.

My stripper name is Geoff.

It's not a very good stripper name
but then I'm not a very good stripper.

My wife thinks I should donate blood.
All of it.

Give your business a family feel by putting
the youngest members of staff's paintings
on the fridge.

I can go ahead and check winning a staring
contest with an Asian baby on public
transport off my bucket list.

My suicide note will be written in my wife's
handwriting.

"You go man! Your dance moves are amazing! Why not get up on stage for some karaoke too! You're an amazing singer!"
— Bourbon

———————————

Some people are as helpful as the "p" in receipt. Actually, at least that's silent.

———————————

"You're the reason we can't have nice things." — Me talking to the mirror.

———————————

The Terminator was easily the best cyber-bully.

———————————

They've released Salt 'n Shake potato chips where you control how much salt you have.

If I wanted DIY chips I would have bought a potato.

———————————

My favourite thing about militant feminists is their boobs.

———————————

A woman on death row:

"What do you want for your last meal?"

"I don't care. You pick."

"Fish?"

"Gross, no."

"Steak?"

"No. Anything is fine."

"Pasta?"

"Ew, carbs."

My laziness is exactly like the number 8.

If it lays down, it becomes infinite.

When I'm standing in line, I only hate the people in front of me. Everyone behind me is cool.

Step 1: Put topics on dartboard.

Step 2: Blindly throw dart.

Step 3: Sing topic over and over.

Congratulations! You just wrote a Red Hot Chili Peppers' song!

If you love someone, set them free.

If they don't come back, text them when you're drunk.

"Let's see how unpopular we can get."
— Politicians.

Be aware that 95% of the time, taking men on shopping trips to buy a valance for your bed ends in his suicide.

How many Vietnam veterans does it take to change a light bulb?

You don't know cos you weren't there, man!

Scottish detectives have identified two suspects in connection with the 1988 Lockerbie bombing.

They don't muck about, do they?

Welcome to Literal Club. Everyone, please take a seat. No, no, put them all back you guys! Ugh, kill me now. WAIT, IT'S JUST AN EXPRESSION!

A woman describing the size of a bug is the same as a man describing the size of his penis.

———————

"I think therefore I am." — Descartes.

"I think therefore I am wrong."
— Any married guy.

———————

Here's to hoping Hallmark makes a sympathy card for shitting in a friend's broom closet.

———————

Ever get drunk and try to see if you're as flexible as you were 20 years ago?

Don't.

———————

I'm sorry I couldn't make it to your party, but this September I was reading Apple's terms and conditions before hitting accept.

———————

The Colour Purple II: Dye Purpler.

———————

I keep telling my wife it's not safe to put on makeup while driving but she still makes me do it.

———————————

Roger Daltrey from the Who has installed wind turbines at home.

Now he just keeps talkin' 'bout his generation.

———————————

Tokyo Disneyland has gone broke. Nobody there was tall enough to go on the good rides.

———————————

We live in a society where people will have unprotected sex but have a case for their iPhone.

———————————

I've just had sex with a lesbian.

Well, she is now.

———————————

I saw a boat on the beach this morning with a sign that said, "FOR SALE"... so I added an 'ing'.

Idiots. Lucky for them I was walking past.

———————————

The start of the week equivalent of
TGI Friday is OFI Monday.

You don't have to specify "Dog, the Bounty
Hunter".

You're the only guy named Dog. We hear
"Dog", we get who they're talking about.

NEWSFLASH!

A man who robbed banks and disguised
as a woman has received a 15 year prison
sentence.

And the judge warned him that his career
as a female impersonator was probably
not over just yet ...

I'm not saying I'm better than you but one
time, I found the right Tupperware lid on
the first try.

I'm wearing a sun visor instead of a cap
because I'm trying to get laid with the
difficulty setting on 'expert'.

Remember, your boss is more scared of you than you are of them.

Wait, that's snakes. Remain fearful of your boss.

No matter how itchy it gets, never EVER try to wash your arse with a paper towel and hand sanitiser. You have to trust me on this.

When women don't want to give me their phone number, they make up a fake number. This one girl says to me, "My number is 3456, 789, um, 10."
Is 10 a number on my phone? Amazing.
She gave me a fake number that contained an actual fake number.

Channel 9 have announced that due to poor ratings *Big Brother* will not be returning.

It feels like the end of an error.

Listen up kids, you can't pick pickled peppers. Pickling is a process that happens after picking.

Mother Goose was a damn liar.

I'm only one Real Funeral Insurance commercial away from taking my own life.

FOR SALE

1 hammer (good condition)

1 TV (some hammer damage)

1 phone (noticeably hammered)

1 dishwasher (hammered the shit out of this, sorry)

My uncle was a mad scientist.

I used to tell him, "Getting angry won't cure diabetes".

I was confident about winning the International Palindrome World Cup.

But then in walked Hannah Tippit, followed by her mum, dad and nan.

Damn you, autocollect!

I wonder if Charles Darwin ever thought that dolphins and butterflies would further evolve into tramp stamps.

Fox News: A man who underwent surgery to look like Justin Bieber has been found dead.

Bloody tease.

I had an embarrassing wardrobe malfunction the other day.

The lock broke and my neighbour escaped.

My wife accused me of not finishing stories.

I got angry and started yelling but then the craziest thing happened.

Under new media integrity guidelines, Channel 9's planned *Celebrity Big Brother* has been renamed *Big Brother*.

I said to the pilot as we got on,
"Do these planes crash much?"
He said, "No, just the once".

I want to be a dog so someone will feed me treats for sitting down.

Have you ever noticed the "&" symbol looks like a guy dragging his arse along the floor?

&

See?

Rich people stay rich by living like they're broke. Broke people stay broke by living like they're rich.

Thump the side of your cat with your palm like it's a dog and the cat will look at you like, "Hey, what's the big idea?!" Funny.

Do you know what you do for a jellyfish sting? Piss on it.

It doesn't work as well on shark bites though. The young boy's family were furious.

There is a fine line between the numerator and the denominator.

Thank goodness for alcohol because these pants aren't going wet themselves.

Velcro is such a rip off.

The best advice I could ever give my daughter is be hard to explain.

How many immature people does it take to change a light bulb?

Your mum.

My wife told me she thinks we're spending too much time together.

I said, "Shhh, you know I can't poo if you're talking".

On our wedding night my new bride said she'd give me a blowjob if I could prove I'd never been with anyone else.

I said, "What's a blowjob?"

Women think men will piss in the sink if the toilet's busy. That's not true.

We'll piss in the sink if it's closer.

I'm not going to do any more jokes about fat people. They've got enough on their plate.

I don't know why all these American rappers always go on about the "West Coast"?

I've been to Perth and it was a shit hole.

I accidentally swallowed some Scrabble tiles.

Going for a poo could spell trouble.

I didn't think it was possible but I failed a personality test.

"What's your favourite vegetable?"

"Stephen Hawking."

"Ummm ... no."

It's comforting to know that you're never too old to completely screw up your life.

I'm not happy with my camping trip travel insurance.

Apparently if someone steals my tent in the night, I'll no longer be covered.

The best thing about having a toddler is that it only takes five times as long to get ready to go anywhere or do anything.

Today I was at the head office of the RSPCA.

It's tiny. You couldn't swing a cat in there.

I bet when prehistoric man needed a coat hanger he just looked for the skeleton of a bat.

I hate it when you give someone a compliment about their moustache and she gets the shits.

My wife and I decided to make our own sex tape.

She was pissed off when I started holding auditions for her role.

What's the toughest part of the Chinese Marathon?

That moment you hit the wall.

Sometimes I ask my farts, "Why me? Why now?"

"Mum! I'm going out!"

"You're not leaving this house until you change that miniskirt!"

"Why?"

"Because I can see your balls, Darren."

———

Great job with auto incorrect, Apple.

———

I told myself that I should stop drinking but why would I listen to a drunk who talks to himself?

———

Statistics are useless. According to statistics the average human has one breast and one testicle.

———

Last night I was pulling my boxers off when my wife walked in and said, "Please don't do that to the dogs!"

———

My indecision is both a gift and a curse.

———

As far as favourite colours, more people like purple than blue and red combined.

I went to aromatherapy. The aromatherapist walked into the room, farted and said that'll be $50.

I've bought eight legs of venison for $40.
I think that's two deer.

Happy birthday, facial burn scars!

My wife wanted to know my sexual history. So I told her about them all. From the girl I lost my virginity to all the way up to her. And that's where I should have stopped ...

I'm not a big fan of jokes that use double entendres and sexual innuendos.
But I do like to slip one in occasionally.

These lollies I just ate had so much food colouring in them, I feel like I've dyed a little on the inside.

I guess you heard about me getting diarrhoea at the newsagent's yesterday.

It was in all the papers.

Have you seen those Pug dogs? I bought one for my ex-wife. And despite the squashed nose, bulging eyes, rolls of fat and being ugly, the dog seems to like her.

Maths made simple:

If you have $40 and your wife has $10, she has $50.

Did I already do my Déjà Vu joke?

I've started a music tribute act called Duvet.

We're a cover band.

Sometimes I watch football holding an Xbox controller just to mess with my wife's head.

My friend said to me, "It's so hard being a single mother when you have no kids and you're a teenage boy".

America's national animal is the bald eagle. That's pretty cool. Canada's national animal is the beaver. Not as cool. And that's also why America and Canada can never become one country because their national animal would be the bald beaver.

I knew my wife was cheating on me when she called and said she was shopping with Carol and Carol was in bed with me.

In my family I was the youngest of three. My parents were both older.

Being funny is easier than being interesting.

I've just been told the clocks go back on Sunday so I'm screwed.

I can't remember where I bought them.

I can't believe I mixed up the Valentine's Day cards.

My girlfriend now thinks I love her and my wife thinks I want to screw her.

To us in Melbourne, Darwin is kind of like the attic. You forget it's up there but when you actually go up there you're like, "Wow, look at all this stuff!"

If your girlfriend says, "I don't want any gifts for my birthday" don't get her any.

It will show you are a good listener. (Don't try this at home.)

My friend loves the desert. I'm a city kid. He's got me out in the desert saying, "Isn't this magnificent"? I'm like, "It will be when they finish it".

I never really knew my mother. She left before I was born.

My family is catholic. All the trouble the Catholic Church is having now, having to apologise to all those kids, my mum says, "We'll maybe this is the change they needed". I'm like, "The Catholic Church aren't big on change and apologies. This is how slow we are on the change wheel. This month the pope went to Russia to apologise to the Orthodox Church for things we did in, ready for this, in the year 1204! That's the file they're on!"

———

I've discovered that when you dig up dead people here it's a crime.

But when you do it in another country it's called archaeology.

———

My friend is a blackjack dealer. On his forearm he has a tattoo of an Ace and a Jack. I'm a blackjack player. On my forearm I'm gonna get a tattoo of a ten and a six. And then another ten.

———

BUSINESS TIP: When shaking hands with a man, don't think about how his hand is never more than a few hours removed from touching his dick.

———————————

Congrats once again to "Shiny, Swaying Thing" for sweeping the Feline Choice Awards.

———————————

I love the woman. I know I love her because she told me.

———————————

I used to be scared of pretty girls until one confessed they were just as scared of me.

———————————

I got into trouble on a date because I didn't open the car door for her.

Instead I just swam up to the surface.

———————————

When life hands you lemons, make lemonade.

Life has never handed me lemons but Syd's Used Cars has.

———————————

Someday, we might make contact with extra-terrestrials but in the meantime I say we enjoy our "alone time".

I just had our ancient family motto translated from its' original Gaelic.

It's "Hey, Get Back in Steerage!"

I come from a show business family.
I was a child actor and my two brothers were child directors.

They say that sitting for long periods of time is very bad for your health.

So now I'm really mad at my high school football coach.

I'm worried because I found out my cholesterol is dangerously high.

My wife tried to cheer me up by making me dinner — bacon cheesecake.

My high school wasn't very good at sport.

We had a big permanent sign in the locker room that said, "We'll get 'em next time!"

Surprise a beautiful person today by disagreeing with them.

Chris Brown said he might retire from music.

That sure is going to leave him with a lot of time on his fists.

The correct serving size for guacamole is "until you run out of chips".

At the Gold Coast it costs $30 per person to go to the Ripley's Believe it or Not Museum.

I couldn't believe it.

At my kid's school the acting teacher quit.

So until they find a permanent acting teacher they've appointed an acting acting teacher.

You kids are so spoiled! In my day we didn't have a wide variety of internet porn.

We had the Myer catalogue and an active imagination.

My wife likes to embarrass me.
The other day at the mall, she had me hold her purse.

Then she went and reported a purse snatching.

There is so much to see in South Australia.

My cousin spent the summer in wine country, then the autumn in rehab country.

If you took all of the George Foreman grills ever sold and laid them end to end, at least they'd be getting used for something.

Remember when you were a kid and you found a PornTube username and password in the woods?

I've been getting a lot of compliments on my rock garden. I've always had a grey thumb.

———————————

COP: "Where were you on the night of the stabbings?"

ME: (not wanting to admit I was watching the *The Bachelor* and crying) "Umm, stabbing people."

———————————

It's a recipe for disaster when your country has an obesity epidemic and a skinny jeans fad.

———————————

My goal in life is to become overrated.

———————————

I swear I don't walk like this when you're not looking at me.

———————————

Normal is getting dressed in clothes that you buy for work and driving through traffic in a car that you are still paying for — in order to get to the job you need to pay for the clothes and the car, and the house you leave vacant all day so you can afford to live in it.

Women are like snowflakes; they're beautiful, no two are alike, and it's very difficult to drive with lots of them on your windscreen.

"How would you like your eggs, sir?"

"Like I like my fighter jets. Scrambled."

I took the kids on a scavenger hunt.

We found two hyenas and a vulture.

My dream is to become famous enough for people to ask, "Hey, what ever happened to him?"

Do you reckon Atilla the Hun's wife called him "hon" or "hun"?

I'm not saying I'm a bad cook but I need frying pans with the non-stick stuff on the outside part too.

Will you hold my hair while I eat a KFC Bucket?

I credit my psychology professor for getting me to stop objectifying women.

I don't remember her name but I do remember she had great tits.

Let's drop it

— people who started it.

Cleaning out our garage I found some old shelves.

What's the shelf life of shelves?

MAN: Hi, I'm Dr Johnson from Doctors Without Boundaries.

ME: Isn't it "Borders"?

MAN: (cupping my arse) Isn't what borders?

You'd think that know-it-alls would know that no one likes a know-it-all.

My wife says being with me is an emotional roller coaster.

She's constantly throwing her hands up in the air and vomiting.

I think newspapers overestimate how much we care about other countries. I'm looking at the paper and there's big a headline: 'Earthquake in China kills three'. So now I'm a bit sad but I'm thinking why did I even have to know that? I bet that didn't even make the front page in China! Am I supposed to think there's some big panic going on over there? I'm sure all over China guys are walking around, "What the ...? Where is everybody?! I'm telling you there's two, maybe three guys not here today.

My cousin is a documentary filmmaker making a documentary about the rising number of documentary filmmakers.

Sports on TV in Israel features something called "Super Schlomo".

I thought I had a morbid streak until I met my wife.

I think about my own death occasionally, she thinks about my death constantly.

I used to listen to loud music when I worked out to get myself pumped up. Now I do it so I can't hear the noises my body is making.

If you give me two sticks, some flint rocks, and a pile of dry leaves, I can start complaining about camping.

Sorry I'm late but my necktie got caught in the hotdog roller at 7-Eleven again.

Instructions for washing fitted sheets:

1) Know how to hold 'em.

2) Know how to fold 'em.

3) Know when to walk away.

4) Know when to run.

When visiting my old high school,
I saw my old gym locker.

I can't believe I used to fit in that thing.

Interviewer: Okay, first off, what would you
say is your best quality?

Me: Patience ... Are we done yet?

I thought I'd get rich teaching my chicken
to talk but only got a couple of bucks out
of it.

The Pope is on social media now. And I
thought I pontificated on my tweets.

A journey of 1,000 miles begins with a single travel sickness tablet.

That which doesn't kill me is everything so far.

I always go with my gut but after some recent bad decisions I hate my gut's guts.

I'm going through an awkward face.

If I were wrongly accused of murder and sentenced to hang, my comedian friends would tell me, "At least you're getting some stage time".

Theme parks are valuable research into the effects of long queues on sugar-filled children, cleverly disguised as fun.

My daughter said she wants to make a lot of money and she's interested in medicine.

Her dream is to sue a doctor for malpractice.

This book I'm reading at the park is a real page-turner. Especially when the wind blows.

It's a shame Captain and Tennille aren't staying together for the sake of the elevators.

It's 2017 and yet people still can't believe it's not butter.

Non-conformity isn't for everyone.

My old guidance counsellor was obsessive-compulsive.

He'd say "my door is always open" then he'd leave and go home and make sure.

NASA say there's no evidence of aliens yet they spend hundreds of millions of dollars trying to talk to them. They've got that SETI program — Search for Extra Terrestrial Intelligence. A long range radio dish sending out messages. Do you know how long it takes for a radio signal to leave our galaxy? 35 million years! That means they send out, "Hello, is anybody out there?" and 70 million years later ... "What?"

I wish I loved anything as much as people who don't know a damn thing love commenting on politics.

It was on this date, 800 years ago, that Lake Titicaca was discovered and named by a 4-year-old boy.

I lost my job. Actually, I didn't really lose my job. I know where my job is. It's just when I got there, there was this new guy doing it.

I lost my girlfriend. Actually, I didn't really lose my girlfriend. I know where my girlfriend is. It's just when I got there, there was this new guy doing her.

If your marriage counsellor asks "What's keeping you two together?" don't say, "Stockholm Syndrome".

My new Asian Fusion restaurant combines traditional Thai cooking with the most obnoxious white people you've ever met.

I play hard to get used to.

Anything you can do, I can do drunker ...

"You call that an inch?"
— Mrs. Inchworm on her wedding night.

This Last Aid kit I bought is pretty useless.

My wife lies about her rage.

"First time caller, long time listener" is a creepy thing to say if you aren't calling a radio station.

There's not even a keg here.
This funeral sucks.

I never understood the term "nuclear family" 'til my 12-year-old started having meltdowns.

Who called them an allergist and not an antisneeziologist?

When you've been married as long as I have, "gettin' frisky" just means picking up some more cat food.

Find out if a relationship is worth pursuing by going to Couples Therapy for your first date.

The older I get the less I feel I need to explain myself.

So shove it.

Head injury? Pfft.

I've had amnesia more times than I can remember.

If at first you don't succeed,
you're assembling stuff from IKEA.

So it turns out a mohawk isn't when you shape your moustache like a bird of prey and now I look ridiculous.

If I had any self-control I'd probably eat that too.

My ex-wife recently told me I run away from my problems.

Apparently not far enough.

Probably my worst fear is being buried alive. Or being buried dead too, I suppose.

Just came back from Kalgoolie.
Nothing out there. Long straight roads.

My mate lives there. His wife left him and he saw her walking away for five days.

———————————

Well, this life isn't gonna waste itself.

———————————

"Wash your own damn baby" I RSVPed to the baby shower invitation.

———————————

Two jokes walk into a bar and spot the undercover police. One shouts, "It's a set-up!"

———————————

When you're going up on an escalator and the guy in front of you farts, I call that a 'smellavator'.

———————————

You can do anything.

Just not all of you.

———————————

When I die just tie my shoes together and throw my body over the power lines in my old neighbourhood.

Call me old-fashioned, but I'm off to party like it's 1899.

I took the day off yester.

Me: "Do you ever get the feeling you're being watched?"

Voice from the bushes: "No".

My new issue of *Kidnapper's Weekly* makes cutting out letters for ransom notes a breeze!

I bought the wrong kind of compass. Now I'm lost in the middle of nowhere drawing perfect circles.

Live every day like it's your last.
Find a nice hospital bed and just lay there.

My doctor just called with my MRI results.
Turns out, I have a pool-shaped kidney.

I want to die at someone else's funeral.
Make it all about me right to the very end.

I'm at a Bob Dylan concert right now if any
of you want me to look for your dad.

The idiot parked across from me pulled
in too far and now their stupid headlight
eyelashes are all tangled up with my car
moustache.

(Spelling bee)
"Your word is 'there'."
"Can you use it in a sentence?"
"They're going to put their books over there."

I just saved a heap of money on a suit by using my wife's credit card and ripping up the statement before she saw it.

This morning, I went to the museum to see their exhibition of Early Man.

I got there at 9am but they'd already closed.

I refuse to take part in scavenger hunts unless they're conducted humanely and people agree to use every part of the scavenger.

I bought a bag of plain rolls for two bucks. And you can get the same rolls but with sesame seeds and they're also two bucks. Know what that means? Sesame seeds cost nothing. But somewhere some idiot's farming them. And I know who that idiot was. My Uncle Frank. Or as we called him, "Uncle Centrelink".

"Hi, I'm Margaret, but most people call me Peg."

"Why?"

"I've never known."

Do what you love and the police will follow.

I'm nervous, but not "someone else has my phone in their hand" nervous.

Sorry I reported your Instagram pic but that was one ugly baby.

Hey I just met you and this is crazy.

Here's my number, I'm very lazy.

Your dog resembles Patrick Swayze.

Do you like daffodils? I'm craaazy

I don't want to peak too soon, but at some point would be nice.

Pretentiousness is my bête noir.

When it comes to turkey, my uncle prefers mashed potatoes to stuffing which is unheard of in the world of taxidermy.

I won a dance contest while waiting
to pee.

Actually, I'd prefer we didn't discuss
why I have a TV tray in my bathroom.

Six million wrongs make a reich.

When we have the war against the
machines I really hope me and my
microwave can maintain a working
relationship.

I never feel better about myself than when
I'm doing the Lord's work; judging people.

I don't like tennis. The depressing thing
about tennis is that no matter how much
you play, you'll never be as good as a wall.
I played a wall once, and that sucker was
relentless.

Do you think eventually there will be
so many *Paranormal Activity* Movies it'll
seem normal?

Quitters never win, but they do get
to go home earlier.

Ivan owns six swords. To calculate how
often Ivan has had sex, multiply the
number of swords he owns by the
number zero.

Witnessing a public break-up is a million
times better than your favourite TV show.

If I can't get your bra off right away,
will you just kiss my neck for a long
time and pretend that it usually takes
a while anyway.

Nothing shakes my faith in humanity more
than visiting a public toilet.

A worldwide bacon shortage is looming.

It's like I've been saying, we need
sluttier pigs.

I'm going to L.A. and I'm going to be staying in Echo Park or as it's known locally, "Echo Park, Echo Park".

I'm paranoid that I hate me.

The main reason I don't use condoms is because I'm not having sex.

It's scary to think I could be dead right now if that Japanese gardener hadn't helped me with my karate.

It's funny how in Neanderthal days they used to be frightened of the moon, lightning and same sex marriage.

I can dance the cancan but only when I've drunk too much from the bottlebottle.

Fashion tip: look bored.

Was Barry white?

Was Marvin gay?

Was Cilla black?

Sure makes Stevie wonder ...

A termite goes into a pub. He says to the guy next to him, "Is the bar tender here?"

Had a bit of back door action with my wife last night.

I came home drunk so she'd locked me out in the yard.

For those of you who don't know how a woman gets aroused, the G spot is located at the end of the word "Shopping".

Just saw two blind men fighting in the street.

You should have seen them run when I said, "My money's on the one with the knife".

Always keep a pen behind your ear in case you need to write something down, such as "I just realised a pen behind my ear looks stupid".

I was just looking at my ceiling. Not sure if it's the best ceiling in the world, but it's definitely up there.

It takes a lot of balls to set up your own Bingo Club.

When someone is murdered, the police investigate the spouse first.

That pretty much tells you everything you need to know about marriage.

"The karma adds 10 pounds."
— Buddhist photographic saying.

The next person that asks me for pineapple juice, cranberry juice, lemonade and a slice of orange in the same glass is gonna get a punch.

I used to date a girl with eczema.

Weird girl but she had a cracking body.

Nobody in a Ford Focus is on their way to get a knuckle tattoo.

"I think we should see other people."
— Eyes.

Statistically, men who tie their hair into a tiny ponytail on top of their heads are more likely to shave their vaginas than men who don't.

I managed to burn 1500 calories in 30 minutes!

The pizza was ruined though.

What's the stupidest animal in the jungle?

The polar bear.

They're looking for a man who stabbed six people with knitting needles. Police say he seems to be following some sort of pattern.

I had a water fight at the park with a bunch of local kids and I won. I think they underestimated me and my kettle.

My mum keeps an empty milk carton in the fridge in case someone wants black coffee.

Why can't Stevie Wonder see his friends?

Because he's married.

I've been arrested. FYI, "holding cells" do not live up to their name.

Not ONE hug so far. This is bullshit.

Do people who do yoga know there's easier ways to fart?

I asked the librarian if they had any books on paranoia. She whispered, "They're behind you".

The boss of Dulux Paints has died of hypothermia trekking across the Antarctic.

Doctors say he needed a second coat.

I went to a day spa today and got a facial mudpack.

I looked pretty good after it but then the mud fell off.

We've got stained glass windows in our house. Bloody pigeons.

I had to have braces when I was a kid because I had big teeth. Huge teeth.

If I had gone to Africa I would have been killed by poachers.

"You wouldn't like me when I'm angry.
Because I always back up my rage with
facts and well documented sources."
— The Credible Hulk.

Just watched an interview with Lance
Armstrong and he lied so much, I'm
beginning to wonder if he ever landed on
the moon at all.

If you want a job in the moisturiser
industry, the best advice I can give is to
apply daily.

Ninety per cent of parenting is being on
Facebook.

Wait, it's not?

(Marty goes looking for his kids.)

And for our next band, would you please
welcome The Repo Men.

Take it away, boys.

I went to a cannibal restaurant. I had the soup of the day and the employee of the month.

I got a sext from a redhead: "I'm all alone. Come over. Bring protection."

I took SPF50.

Making French toast is a lot like making regular toast. The only difference is that you use your tongue.

Did you read how that teacher had sex with her student? Another reason I won't send my dog to obedience school.

Our cat coughed up furballs all over the carpet. I wouldn't mind but Furballs was our hamster.

I was ordering a birthday cake over the phone.

They asked, "And what would you like the cake to say?"

I put the phone down and asked my wife. "Do we want a talking cake?"

If Kim Jong Un launches a missile from North Pyongyang in our direction, I hope the people of South Pyongyang have good insurance.

The pregnancy test we got confirmed my worst fear ... I'm just fat.

I like "insult comics". Last night I worked with a Muslim insult comic. He didn't actually say anything, he just kept throwing shoes at the audience.

The fact that jellyfish have survived for 650 million years despite not having brains gives me hope for our next generation.

I will never divorce my wife because I no longer have enough fart control to start dating again.

I got a tattoo of a Chinese symbol.
My mate asked, "Is it permanent?"

"Yep."

"What's it mean?"

"It means it won't come off."

———————

I took a dip in the hotel pool. The lifeguard said, "What've you got there?"

I said, "Guacamole".

———————

ATMs should have breathalyzers.

———————

I used to mix metaphors but that ship has flown.

———————

I called Sea World.

They said my call would be recorded for training porpoises.

———————